Meet the Artist™

El Greco

Melody S. Mis

PowerKiDS press.

New York

To Evan, Ellsa, and Este Bonnell

Published in 2008 by The Rosen Publishing Group, Inc.
29 East 21st Street, New York, NY 10010

First Edition

Editor: Jennifer Way
Book Design: Greg Tucker
Layout Design: Julio Gil
Photo Researcher: Nicole Pristash

Photo Credits: All background images, p. 6 © Shutterstock.com; cover, pp. 18–19 © Santo Tomé, Toledo/The Bridgeman Art Library International; p. 5 © Museo del Patriarca, Valencia, Lauros, Giraudon/The Bridgeman Art Library International; p. 9 (top) © Benaki Museum, Athens/The Bridgeman Art Library International; p. 9 (bottom) © Museo Lazaro Galdiano, Madrid, Giraudon/The Bridgeman Art Library International; p. 11 © Staatliche Kunstsammlungen, Dresden/The Bridgeman Art Library International; p. 12 © Museo e Gallerie Nazionali di Capodimonte, Naples, Alinari/The Bridgeman Art Library International; p. 15 © Toledo Cathedral, Castilla y Leon, Spain/The Bridgeman Art Library International; p. 16 © Museo de Bellas Artes, Seville/The Bridgeman Art Library International; p. 21 (top) © Metropolitan Museum of Art, New York/The Bridgeman Art Library International; p. 21 (bottom) © Santo Domingo el Antiguo, Toledo/The Bridgeman Art Library International.

Library of Congress Cataloging-in-Publication Data

Mis, Melody S.
  El Greco / Melody S. Mis. — 1st ed.
      p. cm. — (Meet the artist)
  Includes index.
  ISBN-13: 978-1-4042-3844-2 (library binding)
  ISBN-10: 1-4042-3844-1 (library binding)
  1. Greco, 1541?–1614—Juvenile literature. 2. Painters—Spain—Biography—Juvenile literature. I. Title.
  ND813.T4M57 2008
  759.6—dc22
  [B]
                                            2007011808

Manufactured in the United States of America

CONTENTS

Meet El Greco

El Greco is the greatest mannerist artist of the Spanish Renaissance. The Renaissance was a time between the 1300s and 1600s when **classical** art became popular. Mannerism is a **style** of painting that was popular during the 1500s. Mannerist artists painted strange scenes in **dramatic** colors. They also painted people with long, twisted bodies. Sometimes, these artists even included flying animals and other out-of-place objects.

For many years, people did not understand El Greco's art. They believed that his paintings were too weird. Today, El Greco is known as an important painter, **sculptor**, and **architect**.

El Greco's mannerist style of painting is known for its bold use of color. A good example of this style is *The Adoration of the Shepherds*, which he painted around 1605.

Here is Crete, which lies in the
Mediterranean Sea. As he was growing up,
El Greco studied both Greek and Italian
art, language, and history.

Young El Greco

El Greco was born in 1541, on the island of Crete, which is now part of Greece. At that time, Crete was governed by the state of Venice, which is today part of Italy. The people of Crete did not like being governed by the Venetians. The Cretans often **protested** against the taxes that the government in Venice made them pay.

El Greco was born into a rich Greek family. His name at birth was Doménikos Theotokópoulos. He got the name El Greco when he lived in Spain and is known by that name today. *El Greco* means "the Greek" in Spanish.

Becoming a Master Painter

Many painters had begun moving to Crete during the fifteenth century. While El Greco was growing up, he studied icon painting, most likely with one of the artists who lived in his town. Icons are pictures of **holy** people or objects. They were popular subjects for artists who lived in Europe at that time.

By the time El Greco was 22 years old, he was called a master painter. This means that he finished his studies in icon painting and was officially working as an artist and doing different kinds of art.

Top: El Greco painted *The Adoration of the Magi* in the early 1560s. This early work was a lot like the icons that El Greco had started out painting.

Bottom: This El Greco painting is also called *The Adoration of the Magi*. It was painted around 1570. You can see the beginnings of El Greco's mannerist style in this painting.

Art Lessons in Venice

Around 1567, El Greco moved to Venice to study art. He liked the works by the artists known as Titian and Tintoretto. They were two great Renaissance painters who lived around that time. They **influenced** El Greco's style of painting.

El Greco learned how to use dramatic colors when he studied with Titian. From his studies of Tintoretto's paintings, El Greco learned how to draw **elongated** human bodies and how to place them in a scene to make the painting look good. These lessons helped El Greco produce one of his best early paintings, called *The Miracle of Christ Healing the Blind*.

The Miracle of Christ Healing the Blind, from around 1570, is seen as one of El Greco's first masterpieces. The idea for this painting is taken from a story in the Christian Bible.

A Child Blowing on an Ember was painted in the early 1570s, when El Greco first moved to Rome. This painting shows Michelangelo's influence on El Greco's style.

El Greco in Rome

In 1570, El Greco moved to Rome, Italy, where he lived until 1577. While he was there, he studied Roman architecture and the works of Michelangelo, who is thought of as one of the world's greatest artists. Michelangelo was famous for his paintings and his sculptures of the human body. He was also one of the artists who created mannerism.

Michelangelo's influence on El Greco is seen in El Greco's mannerist paintings of people's bodies. In 1572, El Greco joined an artist's guild as a painter of **miniatures**. A guild is an **organization** that made sure its members were paid for their work.

Making Enemies

El Greco became known in Rome for his portraits of other artists. Portraits are drawings or paintings of people. During his stay in Rome, El Greco began to create his own style of painting by using strange color **combinations**.

Some people in the art world did not like El Greco's new style. They also did not like it when El Greco said that he thought Michelangelo was not a good painter. The Italians considered Michelangelo to be a great artist and were proud that he was from their country. Some people were so angry that they quit buying El Greco's paintings.

By 1577, El Greco had made enemies in Rome. Looking for a change and new buyers for his art, he moved to Spain. One of the first paintings El Greco made in Spain was *The Disrobing of Christ*.

15

This page: El Greco painted this portrait of Jorge Manuel around 1600.

Pages 18–19: The Burial of the Count of Orgaz tells the story of a Toledo man who had given a lot of money to the church in which the painting hangs. The painting is made up of portraits of important people who lived in Toledo at the time.

El Greco Moves to Spain

El Greco moved to Toledo, Spain, in 1577. There he had a girlfriend, Jerónima de Las Cuevas. She and El Greco had a son, Jorge Manuel, in 1578.

El Greco's first job in Toledo was to make paintings for the Church of Santo Domingo el Antiguo. These paintings earned him respect in Toledo. El Greco hoped to do paintings for Spain's king Philip II, but the king did not like his work.

In 1586, the Church of Santo Tomé, in Toledo, chose El Greco to do a painting for the church. This painting, called *The Burial of the Count of Orgaz*, is considered to be El Greco's greatest work.

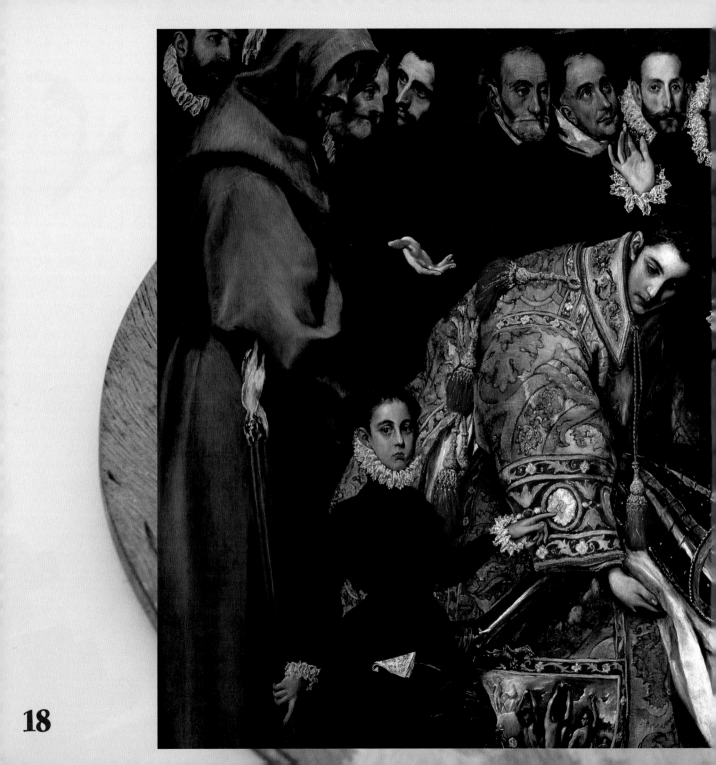

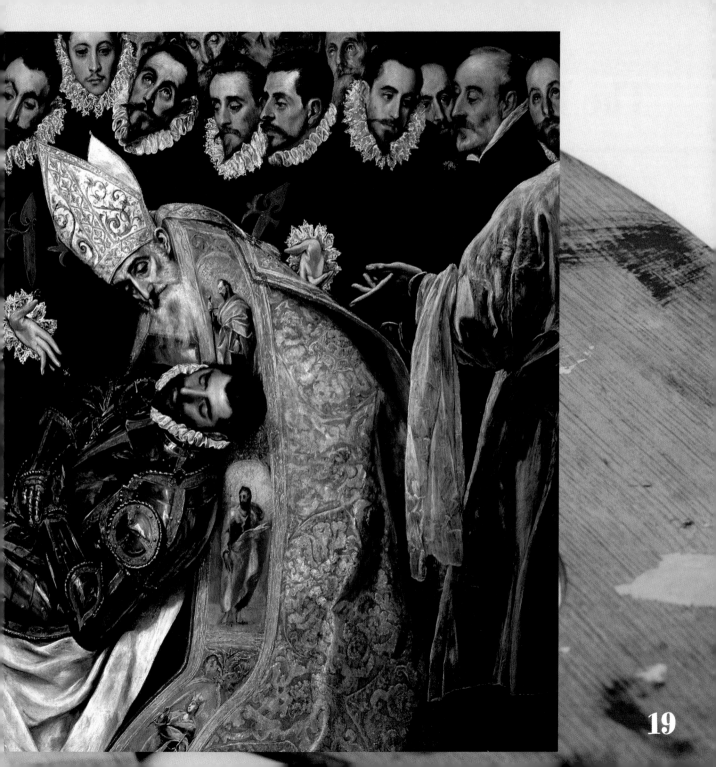

The Busy Years

The 1590s were busy years for El Greco. He produced more than 40 paintings and several sculptures for Spanish churches. He also used his knowledge of architecture to build three **altars**. His paintings were noted for their powerful scenes and weird colors. During these years, the figures in his works became taller and more elongated.

El Greco was making a lot of money for his work, but he often spent it foolishly. He paid for people to travel from Venice to Spain just to play music for him while he ate!

Top: El Greco painted *View of Toledo* around 1597. It shows his idea of what the city looks like using bold, dark colors.

Bottom: This is one of the altars that El Greco made. It is in the Church of Santo Domingo el Antiguo in Toledo.

A Man of Many Talents

El Greco continued working on paintings and sculptures until he died at the age of 73, on April 7, 1614. As he grew older, El Greco's paintings became even more dramatic, with strange shapes and twisted bodies. He believed that colors were the most important part of a painting, and he used them to make scenes appear bright or ghostly.

During his life, El Greco liked to read books and write articles on art and architecture. He was respected as a talented and successful artist in his time, but he was not known as a great artist until the early twentieth century.

GLOSSARY

altars (OL-terz) Tables or stones used in church services.

architect (AR-kuh-tekt) Someone who creates ideas and plans for a building.

classical (KLA-sih-kul) Done in the manner of ancient Greek and Roman art.

combinations (kahm-buh-NAY-shunz) Things that are mixed or brought together.

dramatic (druh-MAT-ik) Striking in appearance and effect.

elongated (ee-LON-gayt-ed) Having a shape that is wider or longer than is often shown.

holy (HOH-lee) Important for reasons of faith.

influenced (IN-floo-entsd) Got others to do something.

miniatures (MIH-nee-uh-churz) Small paintings or drawings.

organization (or-guh-nuh-ZAY-shun) A group.

protested (pruh-TEST-ed) Acted out in disagreement of something.

sculptor (SKULP-tur) A person who makes sculptures, which are works of art made out of clay, stone, metal, or wood.

style (STYL) The way in which something is done.

INDEX

WEB SITES

Due to the changing nature of Internet links, PowerKids
Press has developed an online list of Web sites related to the subject of
this book. This site is updated regularly. Please use this link to access the list:
www.powerkidslinks.com/mta/greco/